ROMEO AND JULIET

William Shakespeare

AGS®

American Guidance Service, Inc.
Circle Pines, Minnesota 55014-1796
1-800-328-2560

AGS ILLUSTRATED CLASSICS

Collection 1

Black Beauty, The Call of the Wild, Dr. Jekyll and Mr. Hyde, Dracula, Frankenstein, Huckleberry Finn, Moby Dick, The Red Badge of Courage, The Time Machine, Tom Sawyer, Treasure Island, 20,000 Leagues Under the Sea

Collection 2

The Great Adventures of Sherlock Holmes, Gulliver's Travels, The Hunchback of Notre Dame, The Invisible Man, Journey to the Center of the Earth, Kidnapped, The Mysterious Island, The Scarlet Letter, The Story of My Life, A Tale of Two Cities, The Three Musketeers, The War of the Worlds

Collection 3

Around the World in Eighty Days, Captains Courageous, A Connecticut Yankee in King Arthur's Court, The Hound of the Baskervilles, The House of the Seven Gables, Jany Eyre, The Last of the Mohicans, The Best of O. Henry, The Best of Poe, Two Years Before the Mast, White Fang, Wuthering Heights

Collection 4

Ben Hur, A Christmas Carol, The Food of the Gods, Ivanhoe, The Man in the Iron Mask, The Prince and the Pauper, The Prisoner of Zenda, The Return of the Native, Robinson Crusoe, The Scarlet Pimpernel, The Sea Wolf, The Swiss Family Robinson

Collection 5

Billy Budd, Crime and Punishment, Don Quixote, Great Expectations, Heidi, The Iliad, Lord Jim, The Mutiny on Board H.M.S. Bounty, The Odyssey, Oliver Twist, Pride and Prejudice, The Turn of the Screw

Shakespeare Collection

As You Like It, Hamlet, Julius Caesar, King Lear, Macbeth, The Merchant of Venice, A Midsummer Night's Dream, Othello, Romeo and Juliet, The Taming of the Shrew, The Tempest, Twelfth Night

Printed in the United States of America
ISBN 0-7854-0811-8
Product Number 40615
A 0 9 8 7 6 5 4 3 2

to the reader

Welcome to the AGS ILLUSTRATED SHAKESPEARE series!

You are about to enjoy a dramatic story that people have been enjoying for almost 400 years. With the help of pictures as well as words, you can find out for yourself why Shakespeare is known as the greatest playwright in the English language. With AGS Illustrated Shakespeare, now you can see Shapespeare's greatest characters as you read about them!

In Shakespeare's day, people enjoyed going to the theater for the same reasons that people today enjoy theater or movies or TV. They liked Shakespeare's colorful characters, whether they were heroes or villains. They liked the action, the humor, and the suspense. They liked story plots that dealt with great human themes, such as ambition and jealousy, love and revenge. In other words, the people in Shakespeare's day liked the same story elements that we do.

The plays of William Shakespeare provide all of these elements and more to readers of any time and place.

Someday you may want to read the plays in their original form. When you do, you will discover the richness of language that makes Shakespeare Shakespeare. In the meantime, sit back and prepare yourself for a great reading experience. We guarantee you'll be caught up in the action before you know it.

—The Editors

about the author

William Shakespeare was born on April 23, 1564, in Stratford-on-Avon, England, the third child of John Shakespeare, a well-to-do merchant, and Mary Arden, his wife. Young William probably attended the Stratford grammar school, where he learned English, Greek, and a great deal of Latin.

In 1582 Shakespeare married Anne Hathaway. By 1583 the couple had a daughter, Susánna, and two years later the twins, Hamnet and Judith. Somewhere between 1585 and 1592 Shakespeare went to London, where he became first an actor and then a playwright. His acting company, The King's Men, appeared most often in the Globe theatre, a part of which Shakespeare himself owned.

In all, Shakespeare is believed to have written thirty-seven plays, several nondramatic poems, and a number of sonnets. In 1611 when he left the active life of the theatre, he returned to Stratford and became a country gentleman, living in the second-largest house in town. For five years he lived a quiet life. Then, on April 23, 1616, William Shakespeare died and was buried in Trinity Church in Stratford. From his own time to the present, Shakespeare is considered one of the greatest writers of the English-speaking world.

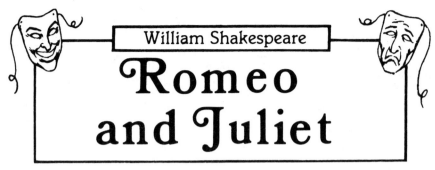

William Shakespeare
Romeo and Juliet

Adapted by
RICH MARGOPOULOS

Illustrated by
NESTOR REDONDO

a
VINCENT FAGO
production

Many years ago in Verona, Italy, there lived two families who hated one another. The Montagues and the Capulets had been carrying on a feud* for as long as they could remember.

If those Montagues should come by, I'll strike before they can run away!

Then take out your sword, for two of them are coming now.

Sampson and Gregory were servants of the Capulets. They were just as ready to fight the Montagues as their masters were.

*a fight between two families that usually lasts for many years

8

As the servants prepared to fight, Montague's nephew,* Benvolio, rushed up to them.

Stop, you fools! You don't know what you're doing!

Just then Tybalt, a nephew of Capulet's wife, saw Benvolio with his sword drawn. He thought Benvolio wanted to fight along with the servants.

Why fight them when you can fight me, Benvolio?

I am trying to keep peace, Tybalt. If you must use your sword, help me to separate these servants.

I do not like the word peace. I hate you and all the other Montagues. Fight me, I say!

*the son of one's brother or sister

people who live and vote in a particular place

Hearing the noise, Old Capulet and Lord Montague came out of their houses to see what was happening.

With this the prince left, and the people went back to their homes.

By the way, Benvolio, have you seen my son Romeo today? I am glad he was not in this fight.

I saw him walking this morning, Lady Montague. He wanted to be left alone.

He has been doing that a lot lately, dear wife. He stays up all night long. And during the day he locks himself in his room.

As they spoke, Romeo came down the street. Benvolio went alone to talk with him.

Good morning, cousin. What is bothering you?

Oh, Benvolio, I am in love!

A short time later, Old Capulet met with the County* Paris, a handsome and rich young man.

Sir, I would like to marry your daughter Juliet.

She is very young. But if she is willing, I will let you marry her.

Come to my feast tonight. You may see some other lady more beautiful than Juliet.

I will come, sir.

Old Capulet called his servant and gave him a list of names.

Go and invite all the people on this list to my home tonight.

*another word for count, a nobleman

At his master's order, the servant took the list and left. But because he could not read, he had to stop someone and ask for help. As luck would have it, Romeo and Benvolio happened to be walking by just then.

Excuse me, good sirs. Can you tell me whose names are on this paper?

As Romeo read the list for him, he saw that the name of the lady he loved was included.*

Thank you for helping me, sirs. My master is Lord Capulet. If you are not Montagues, you are welcome to attend his party.

When the servant left, Benvolio quickly spoke with Romeo.

So your lady is on the list! Let us go to the feast tonight. I am sure you will see others there who are just as pretty. When you compare them, you will agree with me!

*among others

I will go, Benvolio, but not to find someone else. I want only to see my beloved.*

Meanwhile, in the Capulet house, Juliet's mother ordered the family nurse to call her daughter.

Nurse, where is Juliet? Tell her I want to see her.

In a moment Juliet walked in.

What would you like, mother?

I would like to know how you feel about getting married.

*someone who is loved

18

Marriage? I haven't thought about it.

Well, think about it now. Many ladies in Verona younger than yourself are already married.

County Paris has asked for your hand. He will be at the feast tonight. Do you think you can love him?

I will not know until I see him, Mother.

Not long afterward, a servant appeared at the door.

Madam, the guests have arrived, and supper will be served soon.

We'll be right there. Juliet, Paris is waiting. Let us go.

That evening Romeo and Benvolio joined the other guests at the Capulets' costume party. Mercutio, another friend, went along as well.

Cheer up, Romeo. What's the matter?

I had a bad dream last night, Mercutio. I think it was a warning.

Come on. If we waste our time talking, we will be late for supper.

It doesn't matter, Benvolio.

I cannot shake this feeling that something bad is going to happen!

Inside the house, Lord Capulet greeted the masked guests.

Welcome, gentlemen. We must have dancing! Play, musicians,* play!

Some time later, Romeo arrived. Catching sight of Juliet across the room, he asked a servant her name.

What lady is that? She is very lovely.

I do not know her name, sir.

She is like a snowy dove among dark crows. My heart has not known love until tonight!

*people who play instruments

Standing nearby, Tybalt heard Romeo's low words and recognized* his voice.

This man is a Montague. Where is my sword?

Why do you shout so, Tybalt?

Uncle, that man is Romeo, a Montague. He has come here to ruin** your party.

The citizens of Verona think highly of young Romeo. I do not want trouble under my roof, Tybalt.

Bah! You should not allow a Montague here. As you wish, I will not fight him now. But soon he will have to pay for this!

*knew from having seen or heard something before
**spoil, hurt

While Tybalt argued* with Old Capulet, Romeo went over to speak with Juliet.

May I take your hand?

Why not? Saints kiss by holding hands.

If hands can kiss, may my lips do the same.

At that moment, Romeo and Juliet fell deeply in love with one another.

*quarreled

Then Juliet's nurse drew near.

Madam, your mother would like to speak with you.

Very well.

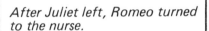

After Juliet left, Romeo turned to the nurse.

Who *is* her mother?

Why, she is the lady of this house.

Her mother is a Capulet. This young girl is an enemy of my family. But I shall surely die without her!

24

Coming up behind him, Benvolio could tell that something had disturbed* Romeo.

Let us leave now.

Yes, perhaps you are right.

As they walked to the door, Lord Capulet urged Romeo and Benvolio to stay. They refused.

We must be going, good sir. But we are glad we came.

When the young men had left, Capulet realized that the party had gone on long enough.

The hour grows late and I must rest. Thank you for coming, everyone. Good night.

*bothered

As the other guests were leaving, Juliet asked her nurse the name of the young man she had last spoken to.

The young man who kissed you? He is a Montague. His name is Romeo, the only son of your great enemy.

My only love springs from my family's hate!

Juliet!

Come, girl. The guests have all gone, and someone calls your name.

Meanwhile, once outside, Romeo could not bear to go home without catching another glimpse* of his beloved Juliet.

How can I go forward when my love remains here?

I must see Juliet again!

As Romeo disappeared** over the garden wall, Benvolio and Mercutio came looking for him.

He ran this way. Call him, Mercutio.

I did, Benvolio. But he won't answer me.

*brief sight, glance
**went away, vanished

Let's go then, Mercutio. We can't find someone who doesn't wish to be found.

Meanwhile, in the garden, Romeo saw Juliet at her balcony * window.

Wait! What light is that? It is Juliet, as bright and beautiful as the sun!

Without seeing Romeo, Juliet stepped out onto the balcony and spoke quietly to herself.

Oh, Romeo, if only you were not a Montague! Yet, if *you* won't change, I'll deny *my* name and no longer be a Capulet!

*a small upstairs porch

It is only the Montague name that makes Romeo an enemy. Take that away, and I would marry him!

At this, Romeo spoke up.

I will hold you to your word, dear Juliet.

Romeo! How did you get here? This house means death for you!

If my relatives* find you here, they'll murder you!

I would rather end my life from your family's hate, Juliet, than die without your love!

*members of one's family

Romeo and Juliet spoke for a few moments of their love. Then Juliet heard her nurse calling at the bedroom door.

I must go. If your love for me is true, tell my servant to-morrow when I send him to you. Then I shall marry you.

I will wait for him at nine o'clock in the morning.

Good night, my love.

Romeo climbed back over the wall. Even though it was very late, he knew he would not be able to sleep.

I will go to see Friar* Laurence and tell him what has happened.

*a priest, a member of a religious order

Romeo, you are up early this morning. Why, I think you haven't been to bed at all!

That is right, Father. Even so, I've had a sweeter rest than you have!

Have you been with Rosaline?

No, I have completely forgotten her.

Where have you been, then?

I have fallen in love with Juliet, Lord Capulet's daughter. You must marry us!

After a few moments of silence, Friar Laurence agreed.

I will help you, Romeo. By joining the Montagues and the Capulets, I may end the feud between your two families!

Early the next morning, Benvolio and Mercutio walked the streets of Venice searching for Romeo.

Where can he be?

I spoke with Romeo's father. He did not come home last night.

Tybalt was angry that Romeo went to the party. He sent a letter to Romeo's house.

It's a challenge,* I'll bet!

And Romeo will fight.

Romeo is as good as dead. If Cupid's** arrow doesn't kill him, Tybalt's sword *will.*

*dare; in this case, an invitation to fight a duel
**the god of love; he shoots arrows into people's hearts to make them fall in love

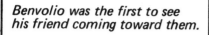

Benvolio was the first to see his friend coming toward them.

Ah, here comes Romeo.

Good day to you both. Please forgive me for running off without you last night.

Just then Juliet's nurse and a servant walked up.

Can any of you gentlemen tell me where I might find Romeo?

I am Romeo.

I would like to speak with you in private, sir.

At this, Mercutio and Benvolio excused themselves.

We are going to dinner at your father's house, Romeo.

Tell Juliet to come to Friar Laurence's place this afternoon. I will marry her there.

This afternoon, sir? She'll be there.

I've told Juliet that the County Paris is a good man to marry, but she won't listen to me.

Good! She thinks only of me!

Tell your lady I love her!

I will a thousand times. Let us go, Peter.

Meanwhile, Juliet was waiting in her garden. The nurse had been gone for about three hours.

Where can she be? She said she would be back in half an hour!

Finally the nurse appeared.

What news is there? Did you meet Romeo?

Romeo is at Friar Laurence's place. Go there, and he will make you his wife.

At this, Juliet hurried away.

It grew very warm that afternoon, and Benvolio pleaded with Mercutio to go home.

I think we should leave, Mercutio. It is hot, and many Capulets are nearby. If we meet one of them, we will surely be in for a fight.

Come on, now, Benvolio. You use the smallest excuse to pick a quarrel yourself!

As they were speaking, Tybalt and some other Capulets appeared. Tybalt was looking for Romeo.

Here come the Capulets.

I don't care. Let them come!

Romeo had just been married to Juliet. Tybalt's words could not anger him.

You have insulted* me, Romeo. Draw your sword.

I cannot fight you, Tybalt. The Capulet name is as dear as my own!

Hearing this, Mercutio thought Romeo was too love-sick to fight. He challenged Tybalt himself.

I will fight you, Tybalt. Hurry, before I cut off your ears!

Then I am ready, Mercutio.

*said or did something that hurt another

*said that something was not allowed

Then Tybalt ran away with the other Capulets, while Mercutio held his bleeding side.

A curse* on the Montague and Capulet houses! I am dying!

Easy, Mercutio. The wound** cannot be very deep.

It is neither deep nor wide. But it is enough to put me in my grave.

Why did you come between us, Romeo? This is all your doing.

I thought it best for all to stop the fight.

*evil wish
**hurt, injury

Help me to a house, Benvolio, or I will die in the street.

Poor Mercutio! This is all my fault. He was hurt trying to protect my reputation.* And I didn't want to fight Tybalt because he is Juliet's cousin.

Just then Benvolio rushed out of a nearby house.

Romeo! Brave Mercutio is dead!

Then I must kill Tybalt, or be killed myself!

*honor, good name

42

Seeing this, Benvolio urged* Romeo to leave.

People are coming! You will get the death penalty** if you are caught!

Benvolio is right. I am a fool.

A crowd soon gathered. The prince himself came to learn what had happened.

Who started this fight?

Tybalt killed Mercutio, and Romeo fought Tybalt for doing it.

*tried to get someone to do something
**punishment

At this, Lady Capulet spoke up.

Benvolio is a good friend of the Montagues, good prince. Do not listen to his story.

But old Montague answered for his son.

If Tybalt killed Mercutio, then Romeo was right in killing Tybalt.

The prince listened to both sides. Then he spoke.

Romeo must be sent away from Verona. If he is caught before leaving the city, he will be put to death.

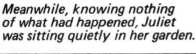

Meanwhile, knowing nothing of what had happened, Juliet was sitting quietly in her garden.

Tonight Romeo will climb my balcony, and we will be together!

Suddenly the nurse arrived carrying the rope ladder that Romeo would use. She was very upset.

What is wrong, nurse?

Tybalt is dead, killed by Romeo. The prince has sent your new husband away from the city!

At this, Juliet was filled with grief. *

If I cannot have Romeo, I will die!

No, Juliet. Do not kill yourself. I know where Romeo is hiding. I will tell him to see you tonight before he leaves.

*great sadness

46

Go and see Juliet, Romeo. Someday Prince Escalus may pardon you. Then you can return to your home.

Friar Laurence told Romeo to leave Verona before dawn and go to the city of Mantua to live.

Just be sure to leave the city before dawn. Go to Mantua for the time being, and I will contact you through your servant Balthasar. Now go.

Thank you, Father. Farewell and good night.

All this time, Juliet's father did not know his daughter was wed to Romeo. He made plans with the County Paris.

I will let you marry Juliet. Then she will forget about her dead cousin.

You may take my daughter as your wife next Thursday. How does that sound?

Sir, I wish tomorrow were Thursday!

I will go upstairs and tell Juliet about this.

At this very moment Romeo was standing on Juliet's balcony.

Must you go so soon, Romeo?

Yes, my love. The birds are starting to sing and the sun is coming up. If I stay any longer I will be killed.

But I would gladly stay and die for you, Juliet, if that is what you wish.

No, no! You must leave!

Just then Juliet's nurse called to her.

She must not find me here! Kiss me, Juliet, and I will go.

Madam, your mother is coming to see you.

I will wait every day for a message from you!

And I will send one, I promise.

With that, Romeo disappeared into the garden and was gone.

As Lady Capulet entered the room, she saw how sad Juliet was and thought she was still weeping at Tybalt's death.

I have good news, Juliet. To make you happy, we have arranged for you to marry the County Paris.

Oh, no! Mother, I will never marry him!

In a moment her father entered the room. Lady Capulet turned to him.

Juliet does not want to marry Paris.

What? You *shall*, Juliet, or I will send you out of this house!

Of course the Capulets thought they knew what was best for their daughter. When she would not do as they wished, they left her room angrily.* Then Juliet found a way to get out of the house.

Nurse, I must go and see Friar Laurence. I have to tell him that I made my parents angry.

That's a good idea, Juliet.

* upset, annoyed, mad at

Meanwhile, the county Paris had gone to see Friar Laurence to make plans for his wedding.

Three days is a very short time!

It is the Capulets who want to hurry.

Ah, it is my lady and my wife.

Just then Juliet rushed into the room. She could hardly wait to speak with the kind friar.

Not yet, Paris. Father, may I see you alone?

When the county Paris had left, Juliet begged the monk to help her.

I know what troubles you, Juliet. And I have an answer.

Drink the liquid* in this vial.** It will put you into a deep sleep, and everyone will think you are dead!

*watery drink
**a small glass tube

You will then be placed in a tomb.* I will write to Romeo, and he will be there when you wake up.

Then you and Romeo can go to live in Mantua.

I'll do it! Goodbye, Father.

Juliet returned at once to her father's house.

Father, I met Paris in Friar Laurence's room. I believe he is a good man.

Then you shall marry him to-morrow instead of Thursday!

Up in her room, Juliet drank the liquid Friar Laurence had given her.

Romeo, I do this to join you!

*a room in which the dead were buried

Within seconds the liquid had done its work.

The next morning, the nurse went to Juliet's room to prepare her for the wedding.

Juliet? Oh, no! She is dead!

Hearing the nurse's cries, Lord and Lady Capulet rushed into the room.

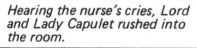

Death has come like a frost to this sweet flower.

Downstairs, the county Paris waited with Friar Laurence.

Is the bride ready to go to church?

She will go to church and never return. Juliet is dead!

While these things were happening, Romeo was walking down a street in Mantua. All at once his servant, Balthasar, found him.

Balthasar, how is Juliet?

Your wife is dead, Romeo. I saw her body placed in the Capulet tomb!

Romeo was stunned* at the news, but he made plans quickly.

Get some horses for us, Balthasar. We will leave for Verona tonight. Are there any messages from Friar Laurence?

No, none.

When Balthasar had gone, Romeo went to a nearby drug store to buy some poison. He planned to take his own life and die next to Juliet.

*shocked, upset

This is enough to kill twenty men.

Thank you, sir. Here is your money.

Meanwhile, back in Verona, Friar Laurence was very upset. The day before, he had written a letter to Romeo and had given it to Friar John. He thought Friar John would bring back an answer.

Have you been to see Romeo, Friar John?

I have bad news, Friar Laurence. The house I was staying in was locked up all day yesterday because they thought someone had a disease* that would spread to others. No one was allowed to come or go until they were sure everything was all right.

The letter you gave me never reached Romeo.

What? Quick, get me some tools! Juliet will wake up in three hours, and Romeo won't be there!

*sickness

At this very moment the county Paris was at Juliet's tomb. Suddenly his servant called out to him.

Sir, I hear horses coming.

Then I'll step aside for a moment. I don't want anyone to see me.

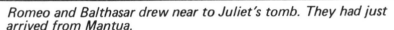

Romeo and Balthasar drew near to Juliet's tomb. They had just arrived from Mantua.

Take this letter, Balthasar, and give it to my father. I would like to be alone.

I will go, sir.

When he had gone, Romeo used Balthasar's tools to open the tomb. Seeing this, Paris stepped from the shadows and ordered Romeo to stop.

Romeo, you killed Juliet's cousin and she died from sadness at his death. You must not do anything else to hurt her family. Leave her tomb alone.

But Paris would not listen. The two men fought, and Paris was killed.

Suddenly Romeo realized that the man he had just killed was Mercutio's cousin. Mercutio had been one of Romeo's best friends.

Now I know who this young man was.

I will lay him in the tomb near Juliet. Then I will join them myself!

Saying this, Romeo picked up the body of Paris and walked into the tomb.

58

Then he drank the bottle of poison.

Just before he fell, he kissed Juliet one last time.

Goodbye, my love!

Moments later, Friar Laurence and Balthasar entered the tomb. Juliet had just awakened. *

Where is Romeo?

He is dead, Juliet, and so is Paris. Let us get out of here at once!

*woke up

But Juliet was too shocked and sad to leave. Meanwhile, Friar Laurence was afraid to be found by the guards, and he and Balthasar left quickly.

I cannot live without Romeo, so I, too, must die!

With this, she took Romeo's dagger* and plunged** it into her heart.

Called by Paris' servant, several guards soon arrived at the tomb. Another guard brought Balthasar and Friar Laurence back.

There is a lot of blood here. What could have happened?

*knife
**pushed quickly

One of the guards went into the tomb and found the bodies. Meanwhile, Prince Escalus and the Capulets arrived.

Romeo and Paris are dead. And Juliet, who we thought was dead before, seems to have killed herself!

Balthasar and Friar Laurence were brought forward for questioning just as Lord Montague reached the tomb.

I will tell you what happened here, Prince Escalus. I secretly married Romeo and Juliet.

I tried to save Juliet from a second marriage by having her pretend to be dead. Romeo was to have taken her with him to Mantua. These deaths are all my fault.

I forgive you, Friar. You only did what you thought best.

At that Balthasar handed Prince Escalus the letter Romeo had given him. It proved what Friar Laurence had said was true.

You Montagues and Capulets! See what your fighting has done? First of all, Mercutio and Paris are dead.

The Capulets have lost Juliet and the Montagues have lost Romeo. All of us have been punished because of you!

And finally, at the prince's words, the two families realized how stupid they had been.*

Montague, give me your hand. From this day forth our feud is over!

I give you my hand and more. We shall never fight again!

That is good! But for now, let us leave this place. The sad story of what happened here will remain with us always!

END

*understood

words to know

nephew
disturbed
glimpse

forbidden
penalty
grief

liquid
stunned
vial

questions

1. How did Romeo hear about the party at the Capulet house? Why did he go?

2. What had Prince Escalus said about fighting in the streets? What was the punishment he gave Romeo when he learned that Romeo had killed Tybalt?

3. Why did Tybalt want to fight Romeo the day after the Capulets' party?

4. How did Mercutio get mixed up in the fight between Romeo and Tybalt? What was the result?

5. How did Friar Laurence plan to help Romeo and Juliet?

6. Who was Friar John? What important part did he play in Romeo and Juliet's story?

7. How did Romeo die? How did Juliet die?

8. What important lesson did the Montagues and Capulets learn from the death of the young people? What did they do about it?